Imaginations 3

Guided Meditations & Yoga FOR KIDS

By Carolyn Clarke

This book is dedicated to Stacie.
I love you a bushel and a peck.

Copyright ©2016 Carolyn Clarke

All rights reserved. No part of this publication may be reproduced, stored in a retrieval system, or transmitted by any means—electronic, mechanical, photographic (photocopying), recording, or otherwise—without prior permission in writing from the author.

ISBN-13: 978-0-9907322-5-9

PRINTED IN THE UNITED STATES OF AMERICA

Table of Contents

Information for Adults 1

Quick Start Guide 6

Breathing Games and Yoga Prep Poses 7

Introduction for Kids 13

Guided Meditations 15

    Tight and Soft 17

    A Bird's-Eye View 18

    Fish 21

    On a Farm 22

    Pumpkin 25

    The Apple Tree 26

    Superhero 29

    Bicycle 30

    Mountaintop 33

    Your Island 34

    Riding a Comet 37

    Moonbeam Blanket 38

    Flying Carpet Ride to India 41

    See the Music 42

    Unicorn Friend 45

    Earth Tour 46

    Peaceful Body, Peaceful World 49

    More Loving Kindness 50

Additional Information & Resources 52

Acknowledgements 53

Information for Adults

The Power of Guided Meditation

This book contains guided meditations for children, and each one is a story meant to be read aloud. Sensory descriptions guide the listening child to a peaceful place. By imagining the sights, sounds, smells, feelings, and even tastes of a peaceful moment, children's brains can make their bodies feel as if they are actually there. Guided meditations can be like a mini-vacation as they calm the body and focus the mind. Most children engage their imaginations easily, making this style of meditation particularly effective and accessible for them. Since most kids are used to having stories read to them, I often refer to guided meditations as special "relaxation stories" meant to help them relax and unwind. I use the terms "guided meditation" and "relaxation story" interchangeably with "story" in this book.

I have used short and sweet guided meditations in my children's yoga classes since 2002. When my students arrive to class, they are often bouncing with energy. Sometimes that energy is positive and happy; other times it is frenetic, anxious, and scattered. Together we stretch, move, and breathe with yoga poses. At the end of the class, I read them a guided meditation, and I see them become more still, quiet, and relaxed with each word. Sometimes, they even drift off to sleep. After they have experienced a guided meditation, their energy tends to be calm and balanced. My students often tell me that relaxation time is their favorite part of the yoga class.

Health Benefits of Relaxation

Reduction in stress ★ Lower heart rate and blood pressure

Less muscle tension ★ Improved concentration and focus

Increased ability to learn ★ Behavioral improvements

Better sleep

Below is a sample of one of the guided meditations included in this book. Experiencing an example for yourself prior to using it with the children in your life is helpful. I recommend asking someone else to read the story aloud to you. Close your eyes and imagine the details, taking time to pause after each question or direction to process the prompt.

Moonbeam Blanket

Imagine it's night.

What do you hear?

What do you smell?

What do you taste?

What do you see?

Now imagine the huge, bright full moon in the night sky.

The sky is filled with beams of bright light.

Imagine that the moonbeams can help you relax.

When their light shines on you, your body feels soft and calm.

The moonbeams shine on your toes, and you feel your toes relax.

They shine on your legs, and your legs relax.

They shine on your belly, and your belly relaxes.

The moonbeams shine on your arms, and your arms relax.

They shine on your chest, and your chest relaxes.

The moonbeams shine on your face, and your face relaxes.

Now imagine the moonbeams covering you like a blanket.

Your whole body feels soft and calm.

Breathe in and imagine your body lighting up brightly like the full moon.

Breathe out and imagine blowing out moonbeams.

Breathe in, filling with light.

Breathe out moonbeams.

Breathe in . . . Breathe out . . .

Enjoy resting and relaxing under the light of the full moon.

Do you feel calmer and more relaxed after reading this story? Did you notice any tension releasing in your body? Did your breath slow and deepen? The children in your life will also feel relaxed after experiencing it.

Using Guided Meditation Every Day

Just like adults, kids need time to wind down after busy and hectic days. Some children struggle with their morning routine before school. Then once at school, they are busy for hours, learning and socializing, often in a very structured environment. This may be even more stressful for an introverted child. Afterschool activities and homework time can add to a child's stress throughout the day. Time to relax is easily lost in the shuffle. However, the benefits of taking time to relax are just as important as anything else in their daily routines, perhaps even more important.

Ideally, children need stress relief throughout their day, and reading them brief guided meditations is an easy way to give them this. Before school, a guided meditation makes the morning routine run more smoothly. Once they are at school, children who hear a relaxation story that engages all five senses are better able to focus and concentrate. Their classroom behavior and grades may even improve. At home, guided meditation at bedtime can help with sleep problems or simply help to establish a relaxing routine at night.

When to Use a Relaxation Story

AT HOME ★ Before school ★ After school ★ At bedtime

AT SCHOOL ★ Before class ★ After recess ★ Before a test
On a rainy day ★ Before creative writing or art projects

AT PLAY ★ During children's yoga ★ Before a sporting event
Before arts and crafts ★ Before writing in a journal
Before a music or dance recital ★ While traveling ★ For fun

Relaxation can help with:

Anxiety and excessive worrying

★

Sleep disorders, nightmares, or being afraid of the dark

★

Autism, ADD, ADHD

★

Depression

★

Low self-esteem or negativity

★

Uncertainty about life changes, such as moving, divorce, death in the family, or going to a new school

How to Use This Book

When using this book, read a single story or a few at a time in a soft, soothing, and slow voice. Remember to give children enough time to not only hear your words, but also process and imagine them before you read the next line of the story. You might feel as though you're reading too slowly, but the listeners will appreciate the extra time.

If you are in a hurry, reading even just one short story will be beneficial. However, if you have time for a long relaxation session, that's even better. Begin with the breathing games and yoga prep poses on the following pages prior to reading a guided meditation. These exercises help the child settle even quicker and deeper into a calm state. Then read the first story, "Tight and Soft," which is based on the practice of progressive muscle relaxation and helps the body relax even more deeply. Finally, choose any of the following, more vivid and imaginative stories.

To make relaxation time even more special, try using a relaxation prop. Diffuse essential oils known to increase relaxation, like lavender oil, into the room. Eye pillows filled with flax seeds and lavender flowers are soothing to the eyes and face and also help children's minds reach inward. Be mindful, though, that what works for one child might not work for another. Children with sensitivities or special needs may not find these props relaxing, and it is always important to check for allergies before using any oils or scents.

If your children and students love these stories—and I think they will—you can always find more in the other books of the Imaginations Series, including *Imaginations: Fun Relaxation Stories and Meditations for Kids* and *Imaginations 2: Relaxation Stories and Guided Imagery for Kids*. Audio versions read aloud by me are available at BambinoYoga.com, where you'll also find art activities that correspond with each story.

Since publishing my first book, *Imaginations*, in 2012, I have heard from parents, teachers, therapists, and other yoga teachers who have been using these relaxation stories with their children and students with great success. I hope that this book is helpful and creates many fun and restful experiences for both you and the children in your life.

Happy Relaxing,

Carolyn

Quick Start Guide

*TIP: Read the guided meditations aloud
in a slow and soothing voice.*

If you have **5 minutes**:
- ★ Read any of the guided meditations (pgs. 15-51)

If you have **10 minutes**:
- ★ Read "Tight and Soft" (pg. 17)
- ★ Read any of the guided meditations (pgs. 18-51)

If you have **15 minutes**:
- ★ Do the breathing exercises (pgs. 8-9)
- ★ Read "Tight and Soft" (pg. 17)
- ★ Read any of the guided meditations (pgs. 18-51)

If you have **30 minutes**:
- ★ Do the breathing exercises (pgs. 8-9)
- ★ Practice the yoga poses (pgs. 10-11)
- ★ Read "Tight and Soft" (pg. 17)
- ★ Read any of the guided meditations (pgs. 18-51)

Breathing Games and Yoga Poses

Adults: Breathing and yoga can be used to prepare children for guided meditation. I use these breathing games and yoga poses in my yoga classes to transition from active time to relaxation time. Breathing exercises help calm the body by focusing the mind on the breath. The yoga poses are slow and calming exercises that are all done while lying on the back. This position activates the part of the nervous system responsible for the body's relaxation response (the parasympathetic nervous system). Lying down for yoga also keeps the child grounded in one place instead of allowing him or her to roam around. Plus, the eyes naturally go to the ceiling instead of around the room, helping the child focus.

Imaginations 3

Breathing Games

Here are a few fun breathing games and yoga poses that complement any relaxation story in this book:

HOBERMAN SPHERE

A Hoberman sphere is a colorful science toy that is also a great visual tool for breathing exercises.

Hold the Hoberman sphere in your hands or let it rest on the ground.

Open it slowly and breathe in. Close it slowly and breathe out.

Keep opening and closing it with your breath.

Fun!

HEART BREATH

Breathe in and open your arms out to the sides, making a T.

Breathe out and put your hands over your heart.

Stay in this position for a moment, then do it again!

Breathing Games and Yoga Poses

Sound Breaths

YAWNING

Take a deep breath in.

As you breathe out, yawn and say, "Ahhh."

Feel your face, shoulders, and neck relax.

HUMMING

Take a deep breath in.

Keeping your mouth closed, breathe out and say "Mmmm."

Make this humming sound two more times.

BUZZING BEE

Take a deep breath in and say, "Zzzz," as you breathe out.

You'll sound like a buzzing bee!

Try it one more time.

Imaginations 3

Yoga Poses

KNEE HUG

1. Lie down on the ground or on your bed.
2. Bring your knees to your chest.
3. Wrap your arms around your knees as if you're giving yourself a big hug.

HAPPY BABY

1. From Knee Hug, let go of your legs.
2. Keep your knees bent and put your feet up in the air.
3. Reach up with your arms and hold on to the bottoms of your feet.

LEGS UP

1. From Happy Baby, let go of your feet.
2. Stretch your legs straight up in the air.
3. You can also do this pose with your legs resting on a wall.

STARFISH (OR "SAVASANA")

1. From Legs Up, lower your legs down to the ground.
2. Leave a little space between your feet.
3. Lay your arms alongside your body, with your palms facing up to the sky.

Introduction for Kids

Yippee! It's time to relax.

Have you had a long day at school and need a little down time?

Are you feeling cranky, worried, or sad about something that happened today?

Or do you feel good, and you want to feel even better?

Relaxing our bodies and focusing our minds helps us to feel happy and healthy.

Guided meditations, or "relaxation stories", can help you do this!

Have fun listening to and imagining the stories in this book.

Each one is an adventure that can take you to magical places.

You'll have a chance to:

- Be a superhero!
- Fly on a comet!
- Meet a unicorn!
- Fly like a bird!
- Send peace and love to the world!
- And lots more!

Ask an adult or friend to read a story to you,
and enjoy feeling peaceful and calm.

Have fun and happy relaxing,

Carolyn

Guided Meditations

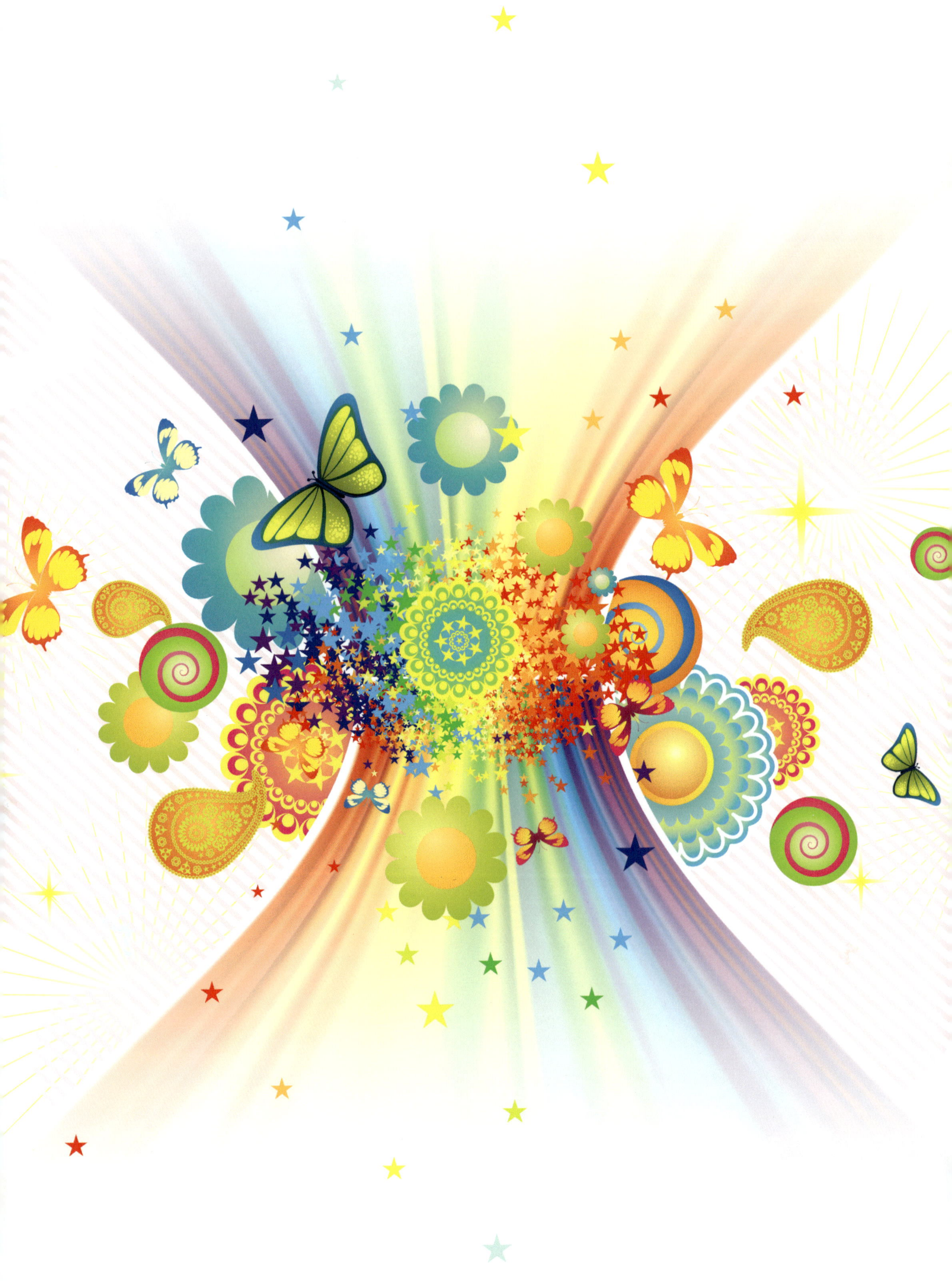

Tight and Soft

NOTE: This story is based on progressive muscle relaxation, which helps a child's body settle into listening and imagining. Try reading this story before any of the others in this book.

Lie down on your back.

Stretch out your legs on the ground, leaving a little space between your feet.

Lay your arms along the sides of your body, with your palms facing up to the sky.

Now you are going to help your body be relaxed and calm.

First, squeeze the muscles in your toes and feet.

Make them tight.

Now make your toes soft and relaxed.

Squeeze the muscles in your legs.

Make them tight.

Now make your legs soft and relaxed.

Squeeze your tummy.

Make it tight.

Now make your tummy soft and relaxed.

Squeeze your arms and make a fist.

Make them tight.

Now make your arms and hands soft and relaxed.

Squeeze your face.

Make it tight, like a raisin face.

Now make your face soft and relaxed.

Squeeze your whole body.

Make your whole body tight.

Now make your whole body soft and relaxed.

A Bird's-Eye View

Imagine you are lying in a giant bird's nest.

Feeling very safe, imagine you become a bird.

Feel your arms becoming wings with feathers.

Imagine you flap your wings and start to fly.

Let's see your life from a bird's-eye view.

Fly over where you live.

What do you see?

Fly over your school.

What do you see?

Fly over your friends playing on the playground.

What do you see?

Peek into the window of your classroom.

What do you see?

How does your life look and feel when you look at it like this, from a bird's-eye view?

Now imagine that you fly away from your town.

Fly anywhere you want to go that makes you happy.

Where do you go?

What do you see there?

Now imagine it is time to fly back to your hometown.

Gently land in your nest.

Imagine you settle down into this cozy nest to rest and relax.

Stay here as a bird in a nest for as long as you wish.

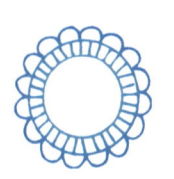

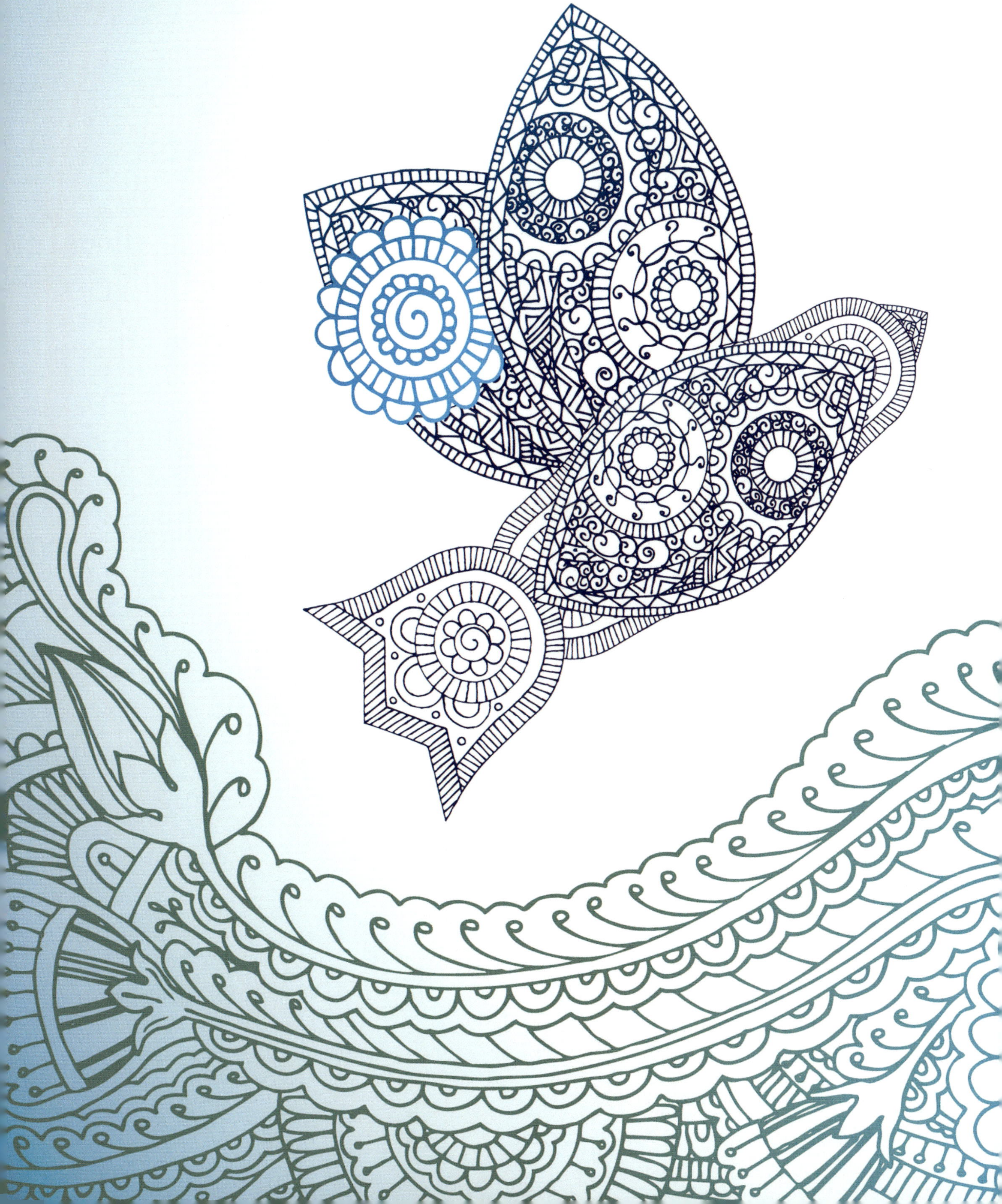

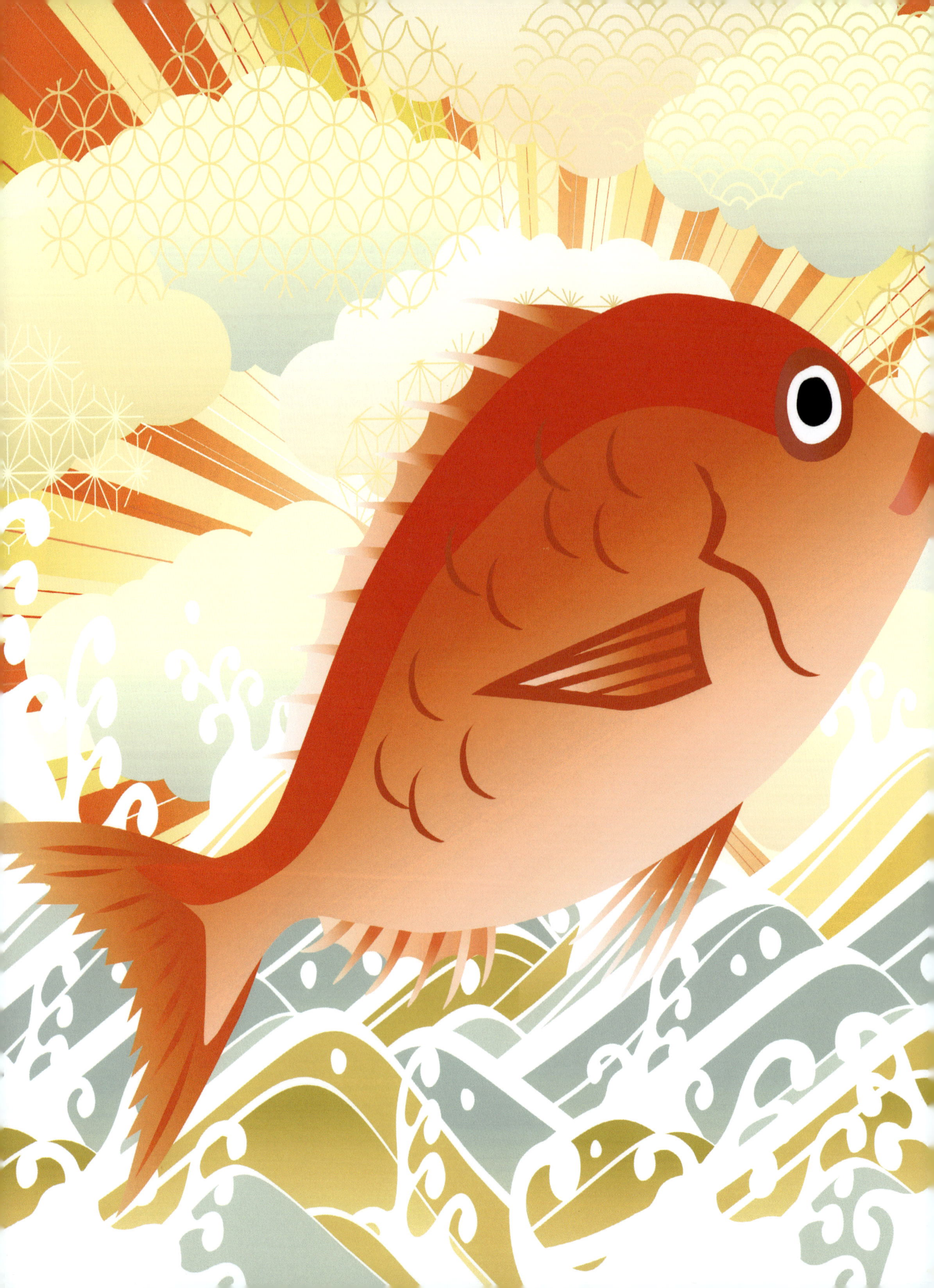

Fish

Imagine you are a fish.

What kind of a fish are you?

What color are your scales?

Are you a big fish or a teeny tiny fish?

Do you have stripes or polka dots?

Are you a rainbow fish?

Where do you live?

In the ocean? In a lake?

In a river or a stream?

Imagine you start to swim.

Feel how easy it is to swim as a fish.

When you breathe, little bubbles float to the surface of the water.

Imagine you can swim anywhere you want to go to as a fish.

What do you do? Where do you go? What do you see?

Do you hear any sounds?

Imagine you jump out of the water.

What do you see now?

Next imagine that you find a school of fish that are just like you.

You swim together in your school of fish, moving at the same time.

Imagine you keep swimming and exploring under the water with your fish friends.

On a Farm

Imagine you are on a farm.

You see a big red barn and a farmer hard at work planting crops.

Do you see any animals?

What sounds do you hear? Cock-a-doodle-doo? Moo?

Imagine you walk to a field of fruits and vegetables.

Take a deep breath in and smell the soil and plants.

The rows of each plant make a beautiful pattern, like a colorful rainbow.

Rows of red strawberries,

Orange carrots,

Yellow squash,

Green spinach,

Blueberries,

Purple cabbage, and any of your favorite fruits and veggies grow here.

Imagine that you pick something of each color to taste.

Feel the crunch of each veggie and the sweetness of each fruit in your mouth.

Imagine that your body is getting energy and vitamins with each colorful bite.

Feel how good your body feels eating colorful, fresh fruits and veggies from the farm.

Send some love to the farmer who worked hard to grow the food to feed you.

Now imagine that you lie down on a bale of hay.

It is comfortable, soft, and a good place to rest.

Take a deep breath in and out.

In and out . . .

Relaxing on the farm.

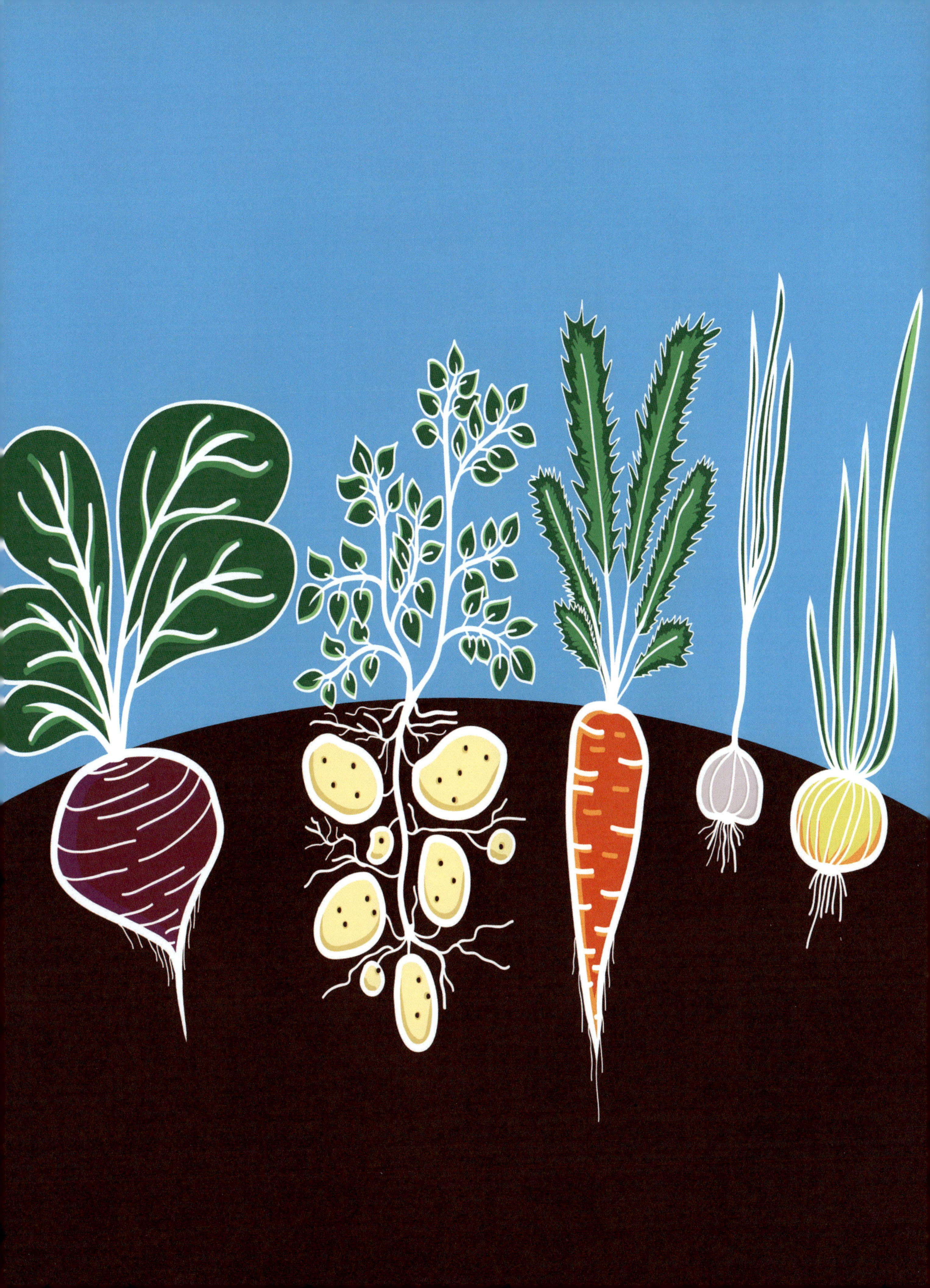

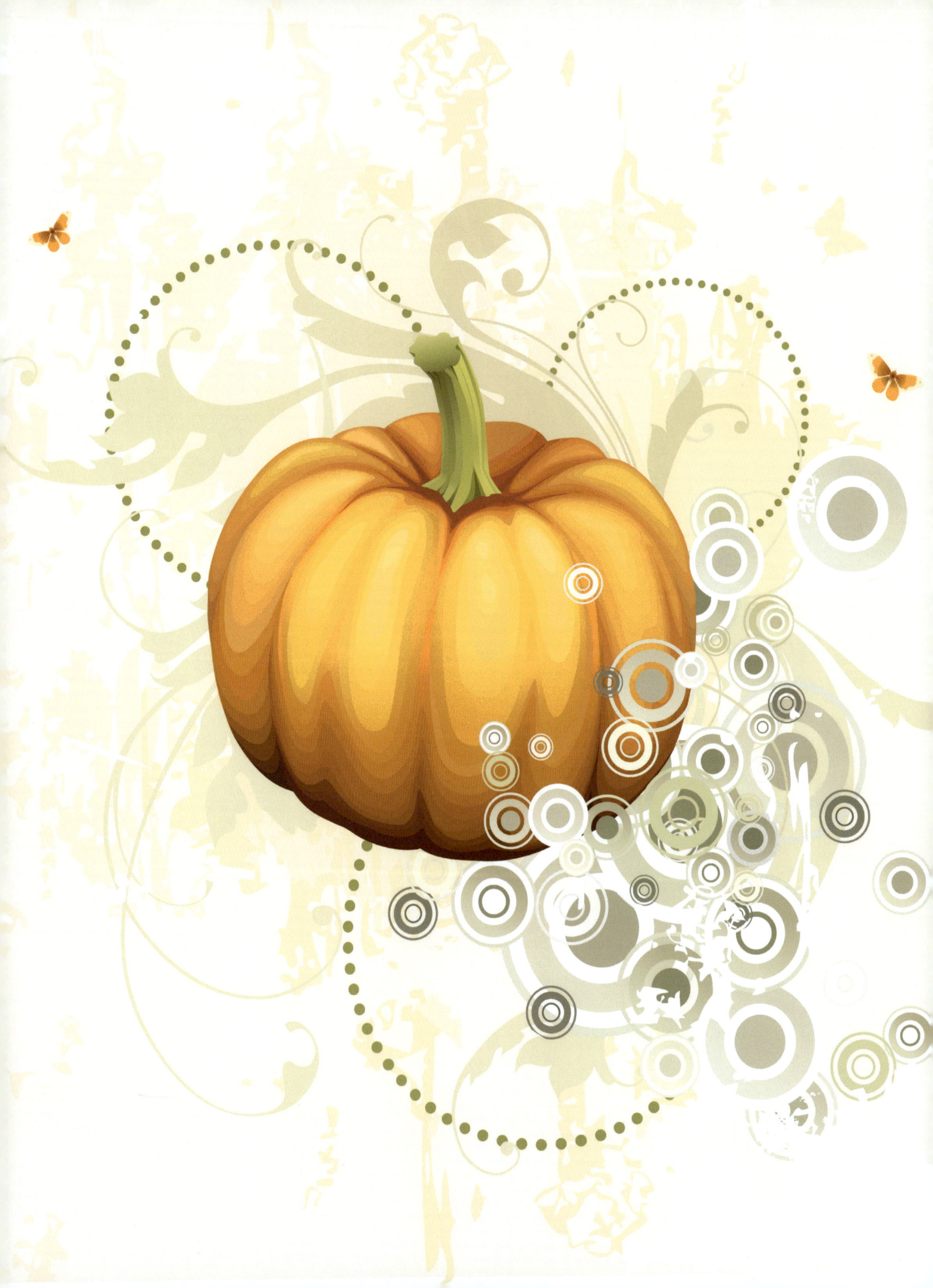

Pumpkin

Imagine that you have a magical seed in your hands.

Whisper a secret to the seed.

Tell it you would like it to grow into a pumpkin.

Now dig a hole in the ground.

Plant your seed in the hole and cover it with dirt.

Imagine that it starts to rain.

Water slowly soaks into the ground.

Now the sun comes out and shines brightly on the garden.

You start to see a tiny sprout poke up out of the soil.

Tangled roots grow down into the ground.

And the seed grows . . .

And grows . . .

And grows . . .

And grows into a beautiful pumpkin.

What color is the pumpkin?

What shape is the pumpkin?

What does the pumpkin smell like?

What is special about this pumpkin?

Enjoy looking at the beautiful pumpkin you grew from a seed.

The Apple Tree

NOTE: *It is fun to eat apples as a snack after reading this meditation.*

Imagine you find the perfect apple tree to climb.

It's not too tall; it's not too short. It is just the right size.

Imagine you reach for branch after branch.

Use your strong muscles to climb to the top.

Look out from your tree.

What do you see?

Listen carefully.

Do you hear anything? The wind in the leaves? Birds singing?

Take deep breaths in and out, to smell your tree.

Can you smell the bark and the leaves?

You see beautiful apples growing all around you on the tree.

What color are they? Red? Yellow? Green?

Pick out one apple and put it in your pocket.

Now imagine carefully climbing back down from your tree.

Hold the apple in your palms and thank the tree for giving you this gift.

Look closely at the apple you picked.

Imagine you can see the shiny, colorful skin of your apple.

Now take a deep breath in and out to smell the perfume of the apple.

Imagine you take just one bite, to taste it.

Is it sweet or tart?

Now sit down in the shade of the apple tree, eating the rest of your apple, bite by bite.

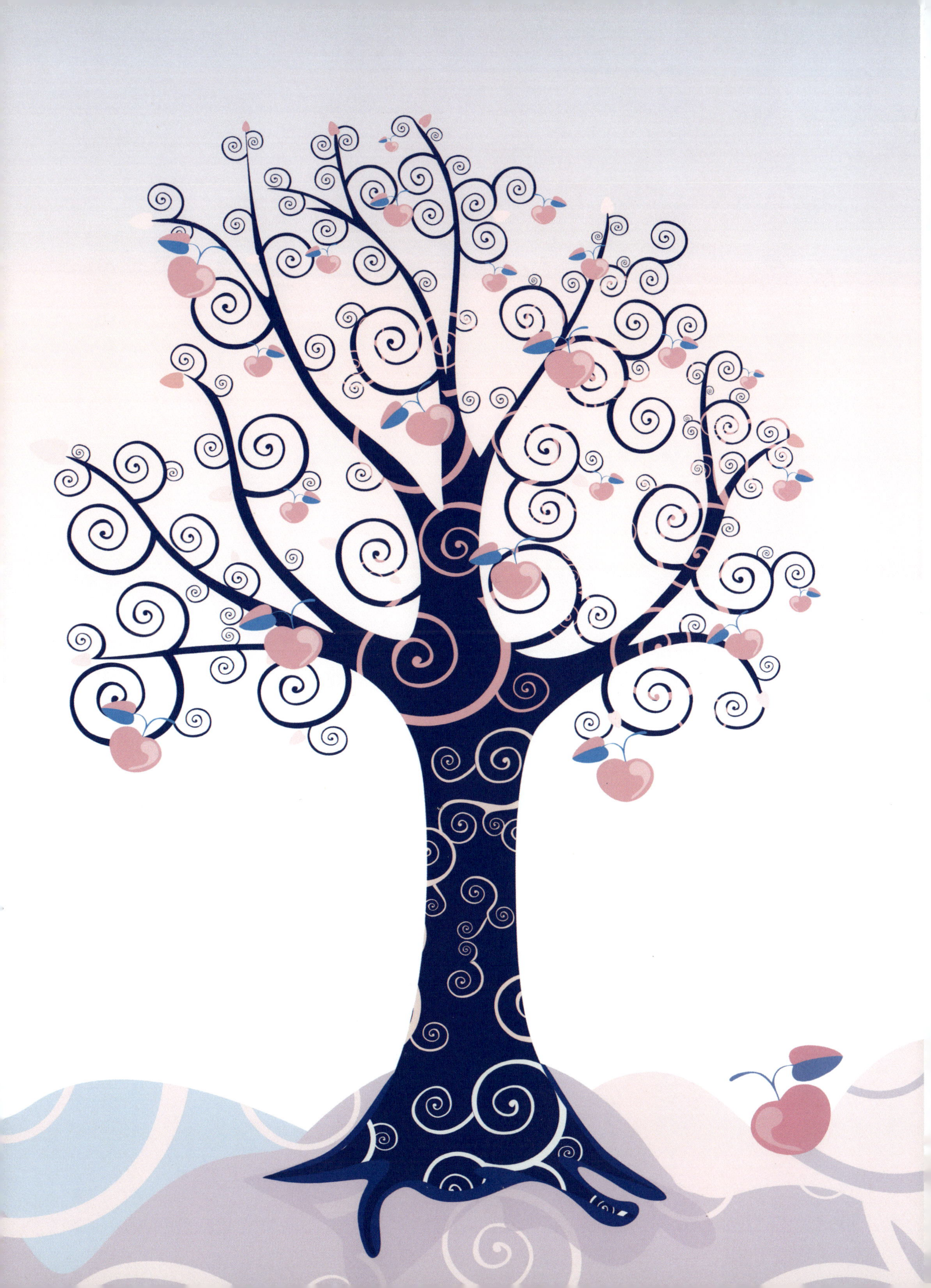

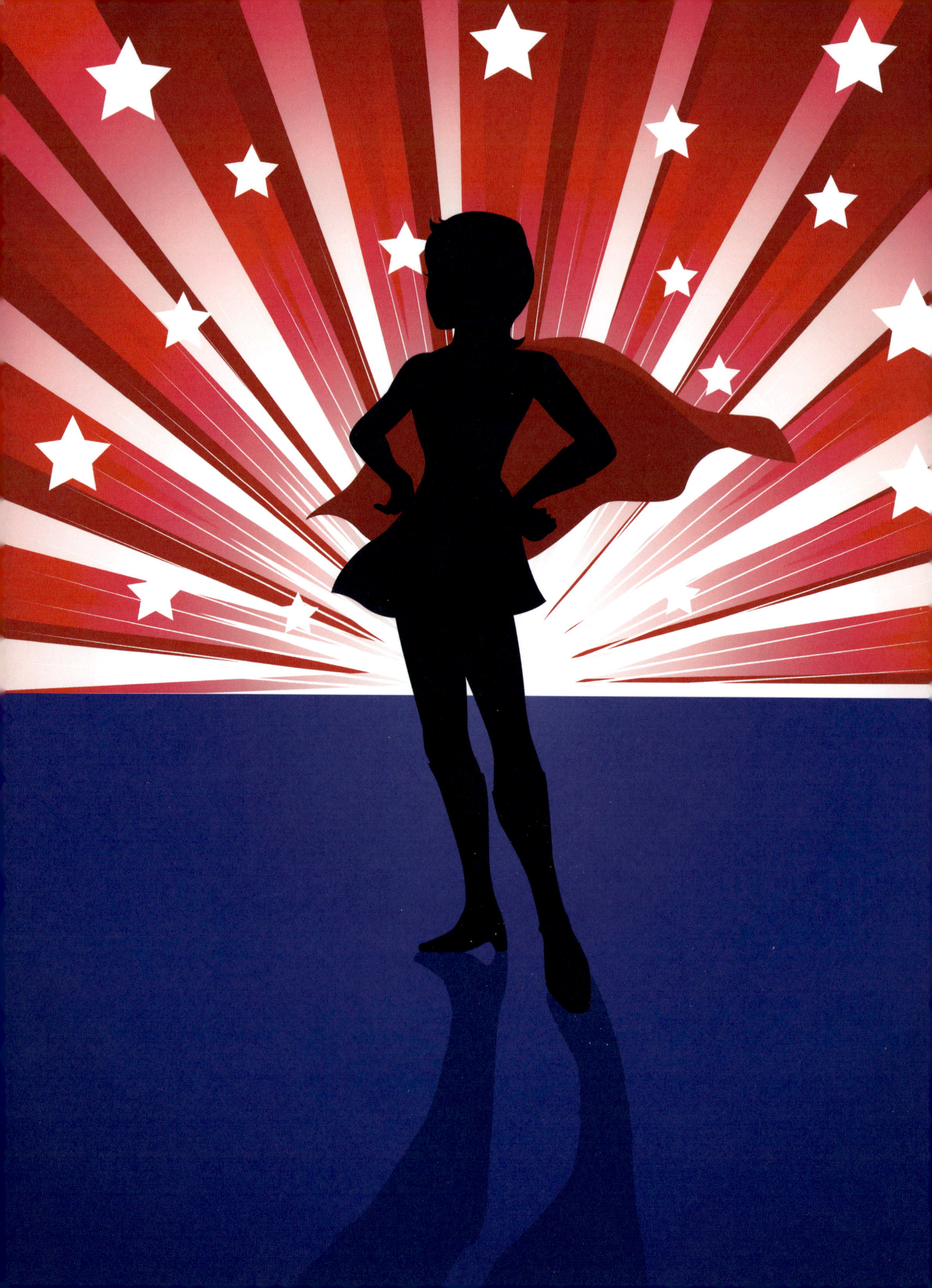

Superhero

Imagine that you are a superhero.

Put on your costume.

Is it a cape? A mask? A full bodysuit?

Imagine your superpowers.

Can you become invisible?

Can you climb walls?

Do you have x-ray vision or super-human strength?

Imagine you have as many superpowers as you wish.

Now imagine how you travel.

Can you fly?

Can you run really fast?

Do you have a special car or plane?

Now imagine using your superpowers to help someone.

Your superpowers save the day!

Where would you go?

What would you do?

Now imagine you turn back into yourself.

You still have superpowers, and you can still save the day.

You are smart, strong, and kind.

Now think to yourself, "I am smart. I am strong. I am kind."

Can you think of more superpowers you have?

Think of all the things that make you great.

Imagine you save the day again,

Just being yourself because you *are* a superhero.

Bicycle

Imagine that you have a bicycle.

What does it look like?

Let's imagine you go on a ride.

Take a deep breath in and out to get ready.

You are brave and strong.

You can ride this bicycle!

Imagine you put on your helmet.

You put your hands on the handlebars and your feet on the pedals.

Imagine you pedal your bike and start to move.

You keep pedaling, and your bicycle keeps moving forward.

Your good balance helps you stay on your bike.

Now imagine the fun you are having on your bicycle.

The wind blows in your hair.

You can go fast. You can go slowly.

You are great at riding this bike.

Now imagine that you ride your bicycle to your favorite place.

Imagine all the things you see along the way.

Remember, if you get scared, take a deep breath in and out. In and out.

It feels so easy to ride your bike now.

Keep pedaling and enjoying your ride.

When you are ready to stop, use the brakes to slow down.

Get off your bike and take off your helmet.

Lie down next to your bicycle and take a rest after your fun bike ride.

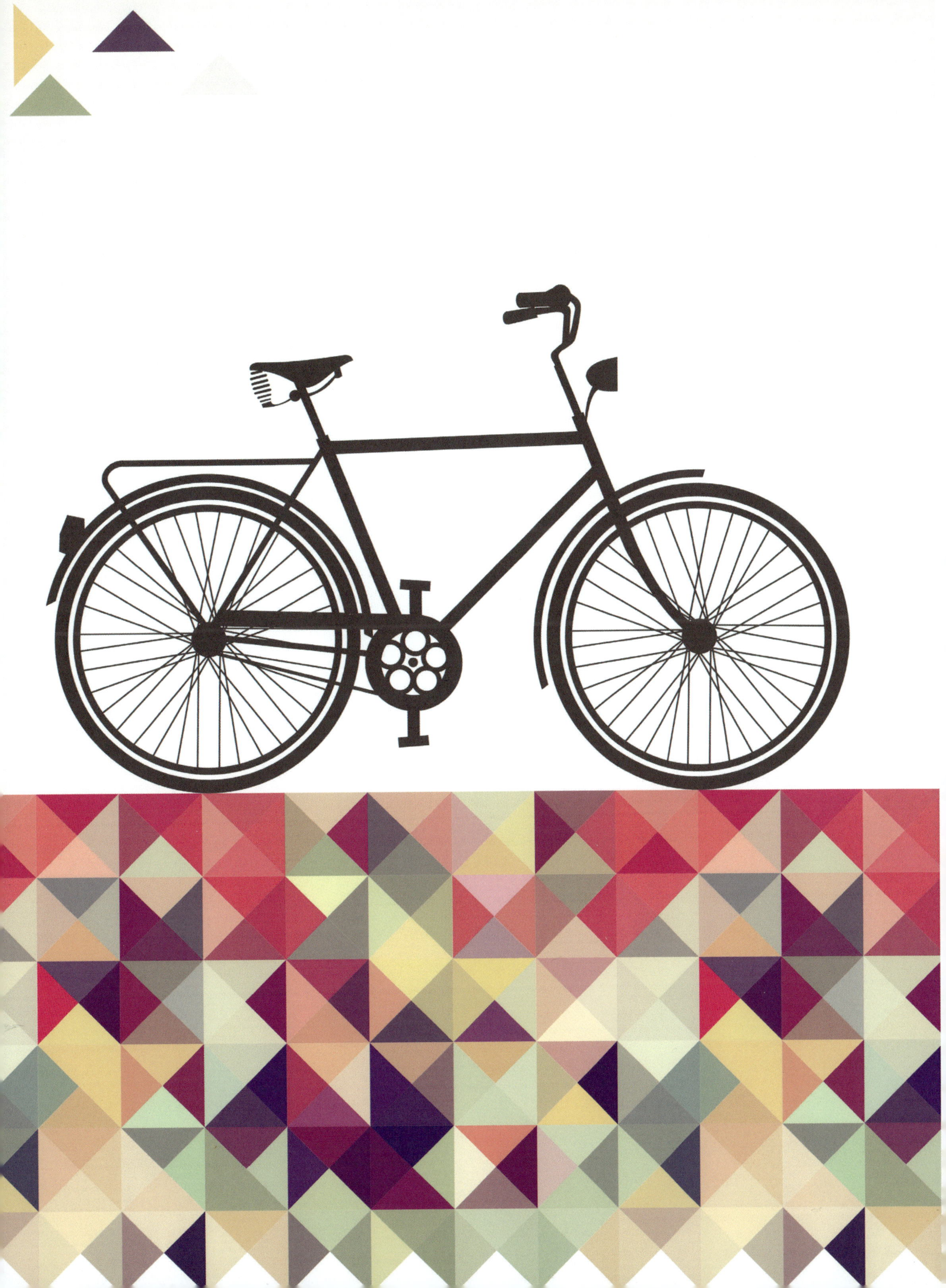

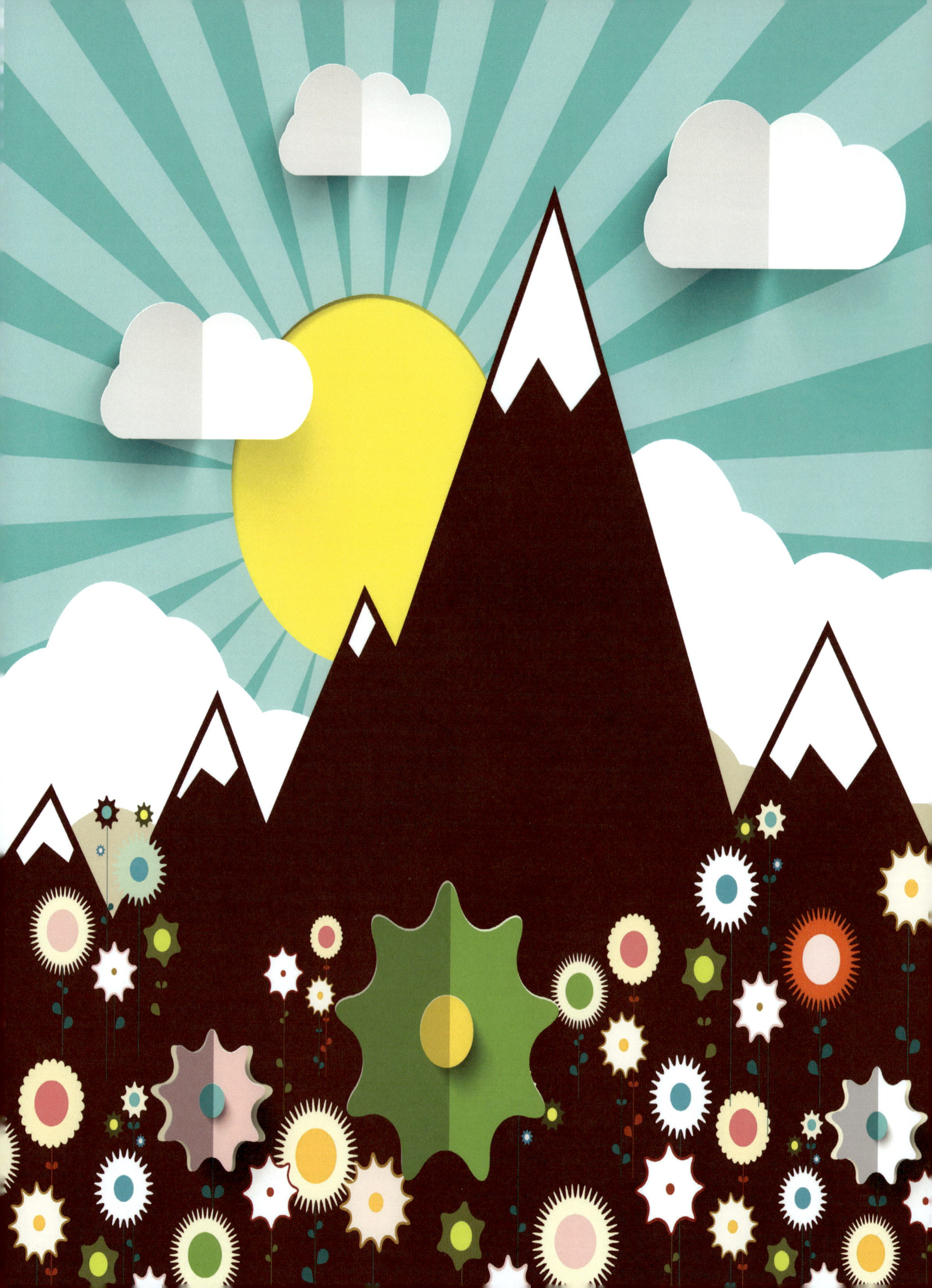

Mountaintop

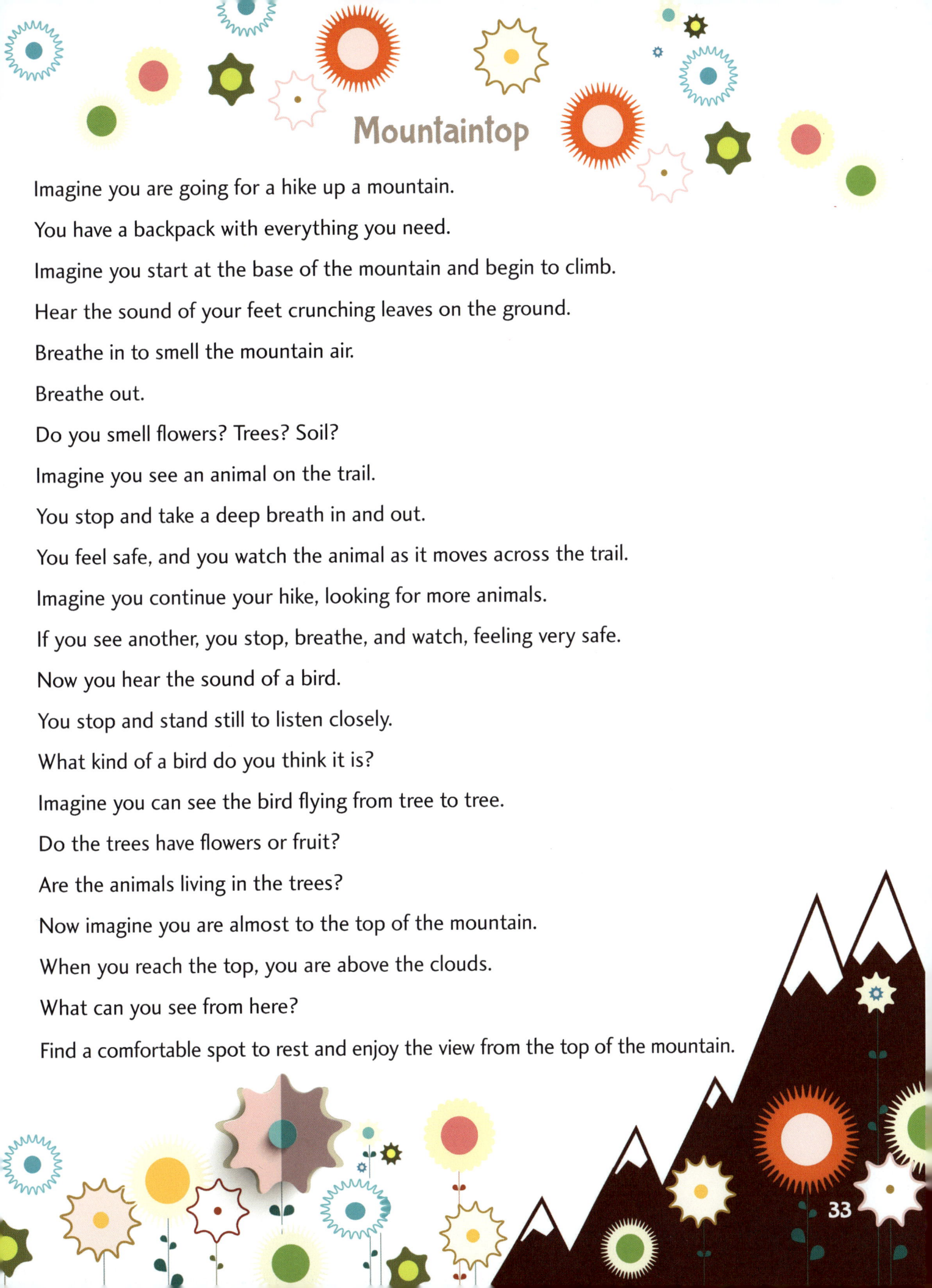

Imagine you are going for a hike up a mountain.

You have a backpack with everything you need.

Imagine you start at the base of the mountain and begin to climb.

Hear the sound of your feet crunching leaves on the ground.

Breathe in to smell the mountain air.

Breathe out.

Do you smell flowers? Trees? Soil?

Imagine you see an animal on the trail.

You stop and take a deep breath in and out.

You feel safe, and you watch the animal as it moves across the trail.

Imagine you continue your hike, looking for more animals.

If you see another, you stop, breathe, and watch, feeling very safe.

Now you hear the sound of a bird.

You stop and stand still to listen closely.

What kind of a bird do you think it is?

Imagine you can see the bird flying from tree to tree.

Do the trees have flowers or fruit?

Are the animals living in the trees?

Now imagine you are almost to the top of the mountain.

When you reach the top, you are above the clouds.

What can you see from here?

Find a comfortable spot to rest and enjoy the view from the top of the mountain.

Your Island

Imagine you are on a boat.

What kind of boat is it?

A sailboat? A motorboat? A pirate ship?

Imagine you go for an adventure on your boat.

You can feel the wind on your face and in your hair.

You can hear water splashing against the boat.

You feel safe, relaxed, and happy.

Now imagine you see land in the distance.

It is a small island.

Imagine you travel there and drop your anchor.

This is your very own island, for you to explore.

What do you see? What do you hear?

What do you smell? What do you taste?

How do you feel?

Now imagine you find a comfortable resting spot on your island,

Maybe under a palm tree or in some soft sand.

Feel your body relax into the ground.

You are safe here.

Everything is just right.

Now imagine you get back into your boat and travel home.

You can come back to your own island any time you wish.

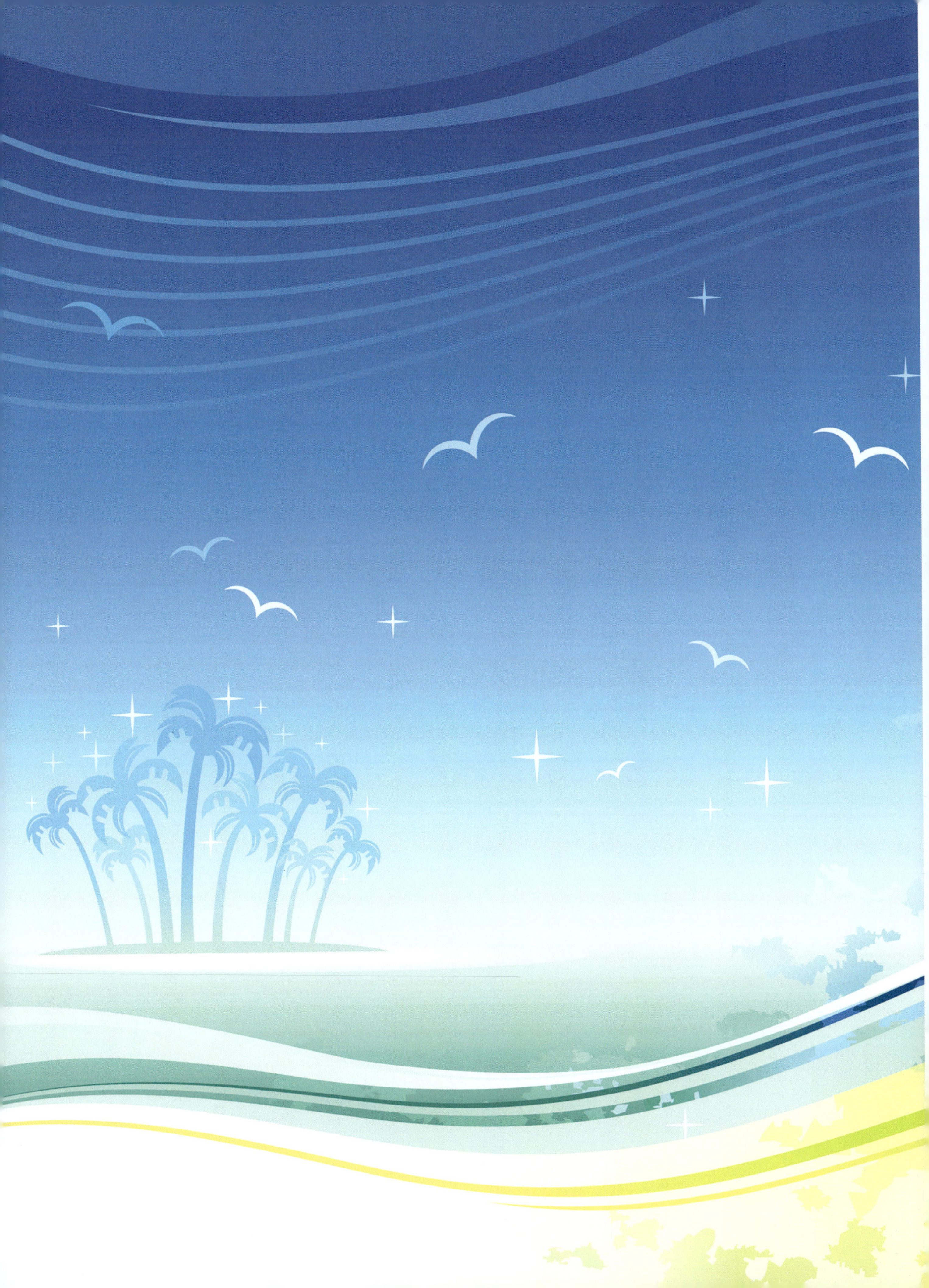

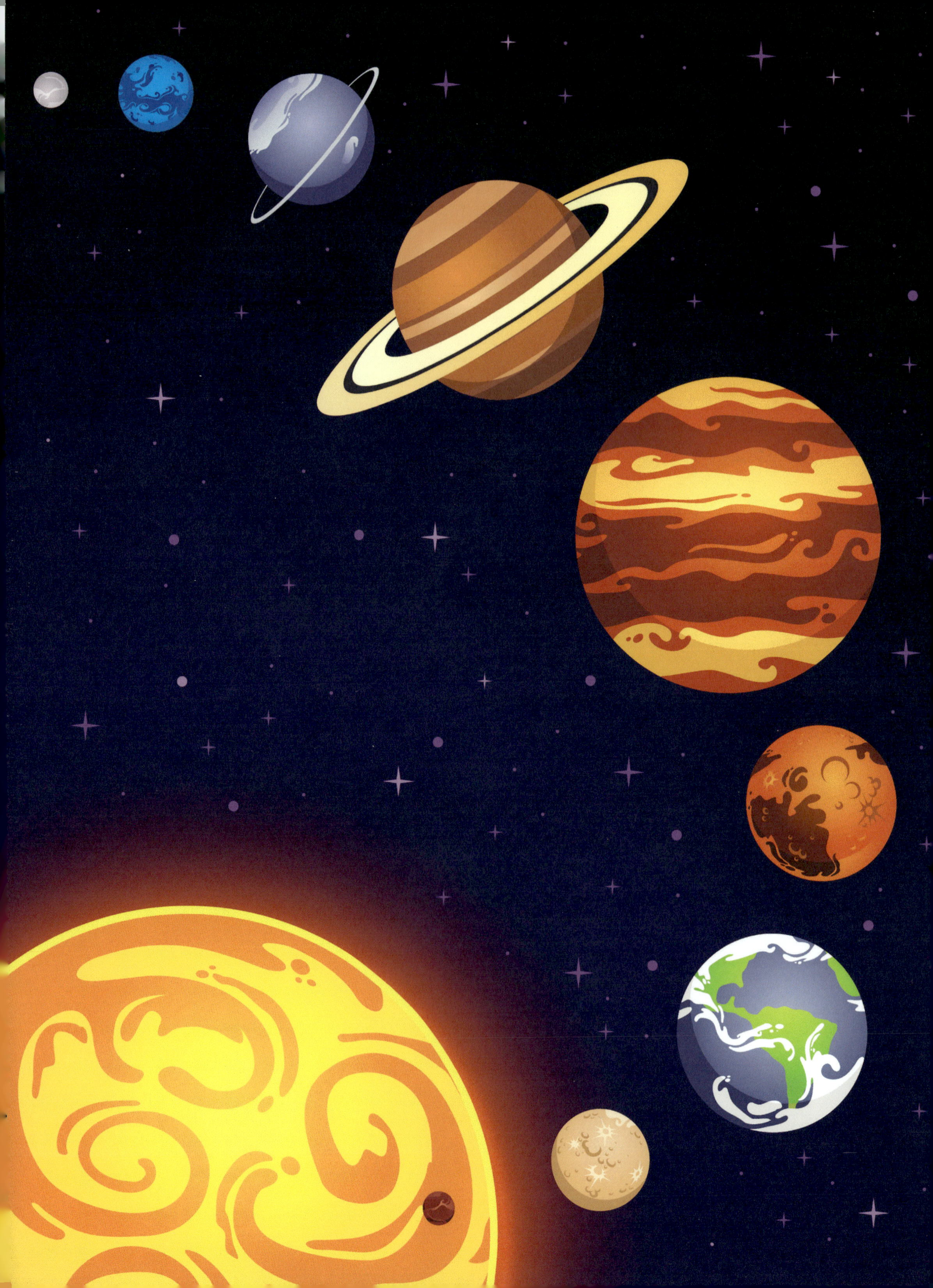

Riding a Comet

Imagine you are going to explore space on a comet.

You put on a spacesuit and get into a spaceship.

Ten . . . nine . . . eight . . . seven . . . six . . . five . . . four . . . three . . . two . . . one . . .

Blastoff! Fly your spaceship and land on a comet.

Imagine you travel on the comet around the Solar System.

You can see our star, the Sun, shining brightly with fire and light.

Your comet flies by Mercury, the first planet next to the sun.

Next your comet flies by the hottest planet, Venus. Can you feel its heat?

You travel past planet Earth, our home with blue water and swirling white clouds.

You zoom by Mars and notice this planet is very red.

You fly past Jupiter, and you see the beautiful swirls and colors of this planet.

Your comet travels past a planet with huge rings made of ice. This is Saturn.

As you fly by the planet Uranus, you notice it has some rings, too.

Next you go past a bright-blue planet, Neptune.

The comet even travels as far as Pluto, the tiny dwarf planet.

Now count your breaths again to launch your spaceship.

Breathe in, and then breathe out and think to yourself, "Ten."
Breathe in, breathe out. "Nine . . ."
Breathe in, breathe out. "Eight . . ."
Breathe in, breathe out. "Seven . . ."
Breathe in, breathe out. "Six . . ."
Breathe in, breathe out. "Five . . ."
Breathe in, breathe out. "Four . . ."
Breathe in, breathe out. "Three . . ."
Breathe in, breathe out. "Two . . ."
Breathe in, breathe out. "One . . ."

Enjoy flying back to Earth in your spaceship, feeling relaxed and calm.

Moonbeam Blanket

Imagine it's night.

What do you hear?

What do you smell?

What do you taste?

What do you see?

Now imagine you see the huge, bright full moon in the night sky.

The sky is filled with beams of bright light.

Imagine that the moonbeams can help you relax.

When their light shines on you, your body feels soft and calm.

The moonbeams shine on your toes, and you feel your toes relax.

They shine on your legs, and your legs relax.

They shine on your belly, and your belly relaxes.

The moonbeams shine on your arms, and your arms relax.

They shine on your chest, and your chest relaxes.

The moonbeams shine on your face, and your face relaxes.

Now imagine the moonbeams covering you like a blanket.

Your whole body feels soft and calm.

Breathe in and imagine your body lighting up brightly like the full moon.

Breathe out and imagine blowing out moonbeams.

Breathe in, filling with light.

Breathe out moonbeams.

Breathe in . . .

Breathe out . . .

Enjoy resting and relaxing under the light of the full moon.

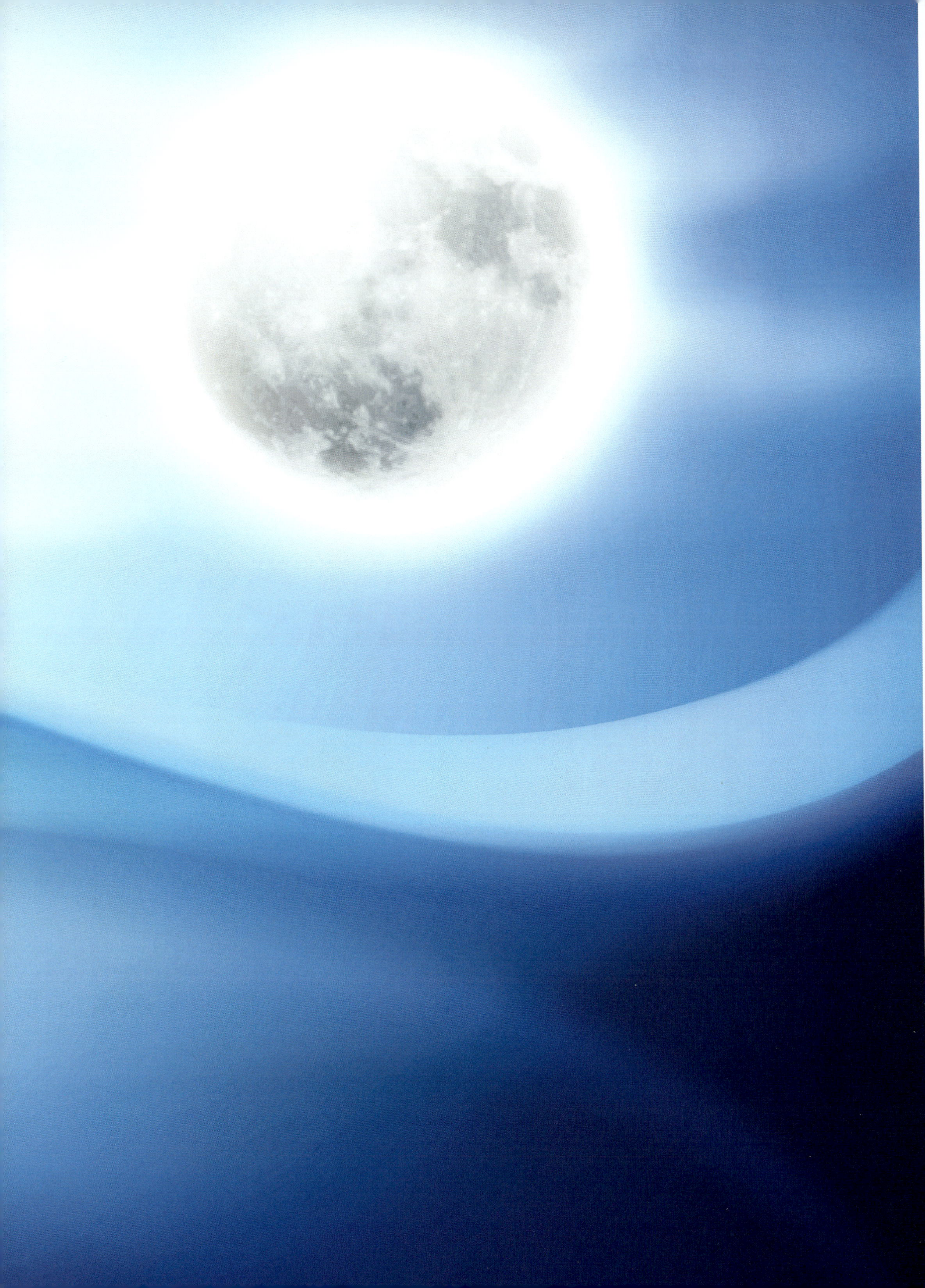

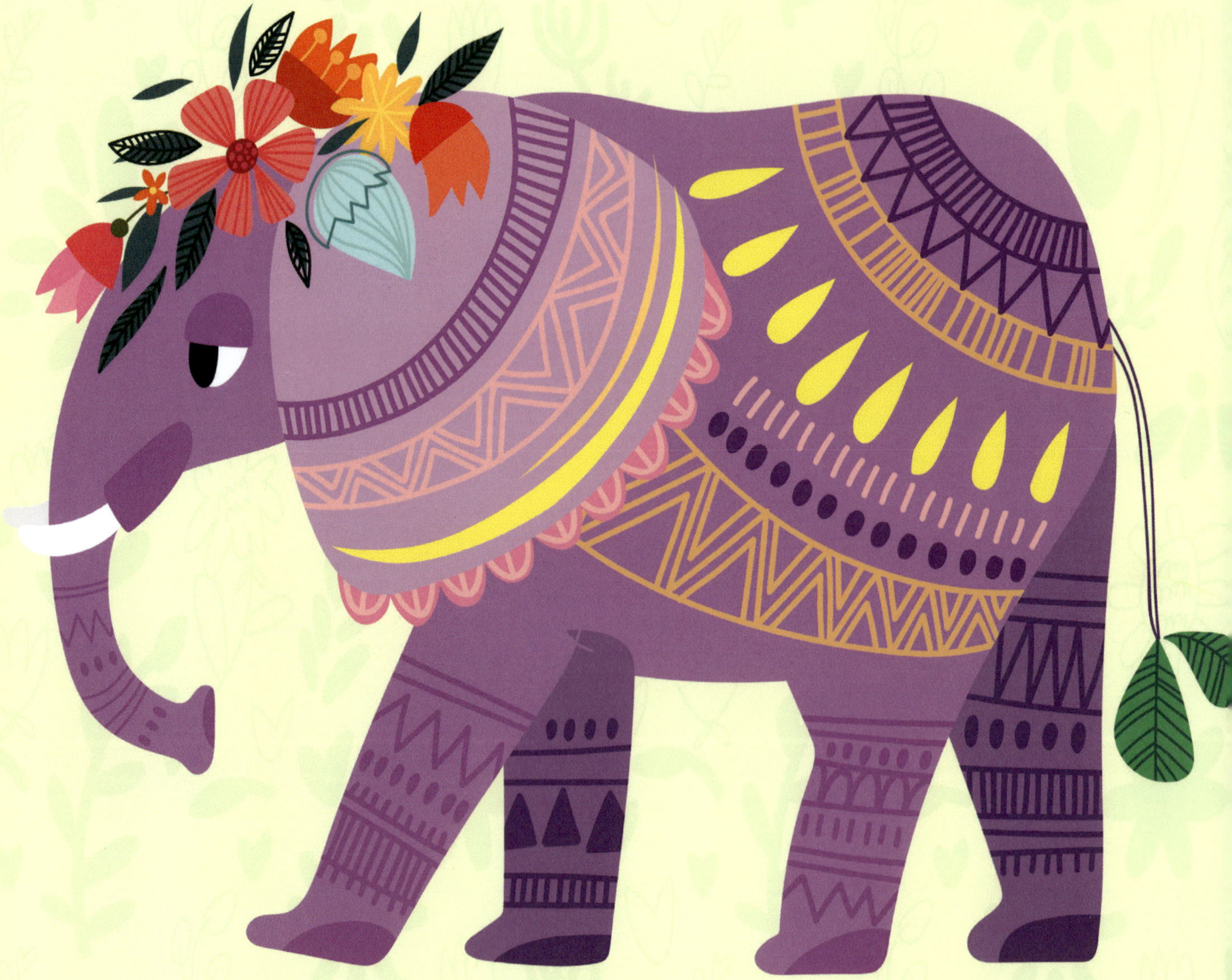

Flying Carpet Ride to India

Imagine you have a flying carpet.

Lie down on the carpet. It feels soft and fluffy against your skin.

Now imagine that your flying carpet will move when you ask it to move.

It will stop when you ask it to stop.

Feeling very safe, you ask your carpet to fly to India.

If you don't know where India is, that's okay, because your flying carpet knows.

Feel your carpet rising up from the ground and starting to fly.

On your carpet, you travel over oceans and land.

Your carpet begins to slow down when you arrive in India.

Ask it to gently float to the ground and land.

Take a look all around you.

The people are wearing brightly colored clothes—oranges, pinks, and reds.

Take a deep breath in and out.

The scent of curry, cinnamon, and lemons fill the air.

These smells are so strong that you can taste them.

When you listen, you hear the sound of a person playing the sitar and children laughing.

You see a man walking with an elephant.

The elephant is decorated with face paint.

Colorful flowers, stars, and swirls decorate his skin.

You look into the elephant's eye as he passes you, and you imagine seeing him smile at you.

Imagine you see people doing yoga.

They stretch and shape their bodies into poses that look like animals and trees.

Take a minute to remember everything that you see, taste, smell, hear, and feel in India.

Now imagine climbing back onto your flying carpet.

Ask your carpet to take off and then feel it gently land on the ground at home.

See the Music

Imagine that you hear the most beautiful music in the world.

It can be any kind of music you wish.

Imagine you can see the instruments playing the sounds of the music.

Hear the sound of the music filling the room.

Now imagine choosing an instrument to play.

Imagine playing along with this beautiful music.

Your body knows just what to do to play this instrument.

Now imagine that you can see the sounds of the music.

Perhaps you can see musical notes dancing out of the instruments and around the room.

Now imagine that you can smell the music.

Maybe the music smells like flowers, vanilla, or lemons.

Now imagine that you can taste the music.

Does it taste spicy? Sweet? Salty?

Imagine that your body can feel the music.

The feeling of the music helps your body relax.

Feel the music on your toes, and feel your toes relax.

Feel the music on your legs, and feel your legs relax.

Feel the music on your belly, and feel your belly relax.

Feel the music on your arms, and feel your arms relax.

Feel the music on your chest, and feel your chest relax.

Feel the music on your face, and feel your face relax.

The music relaxes your whole body.

Now imagine you can drink the music by breathing in and breathing out.

Breathe in and feel the music fill your whole body.

Breathe out and feel the music fill the room.

Breathe in, and breathe out, relaxing with the music.

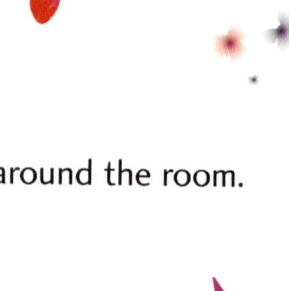

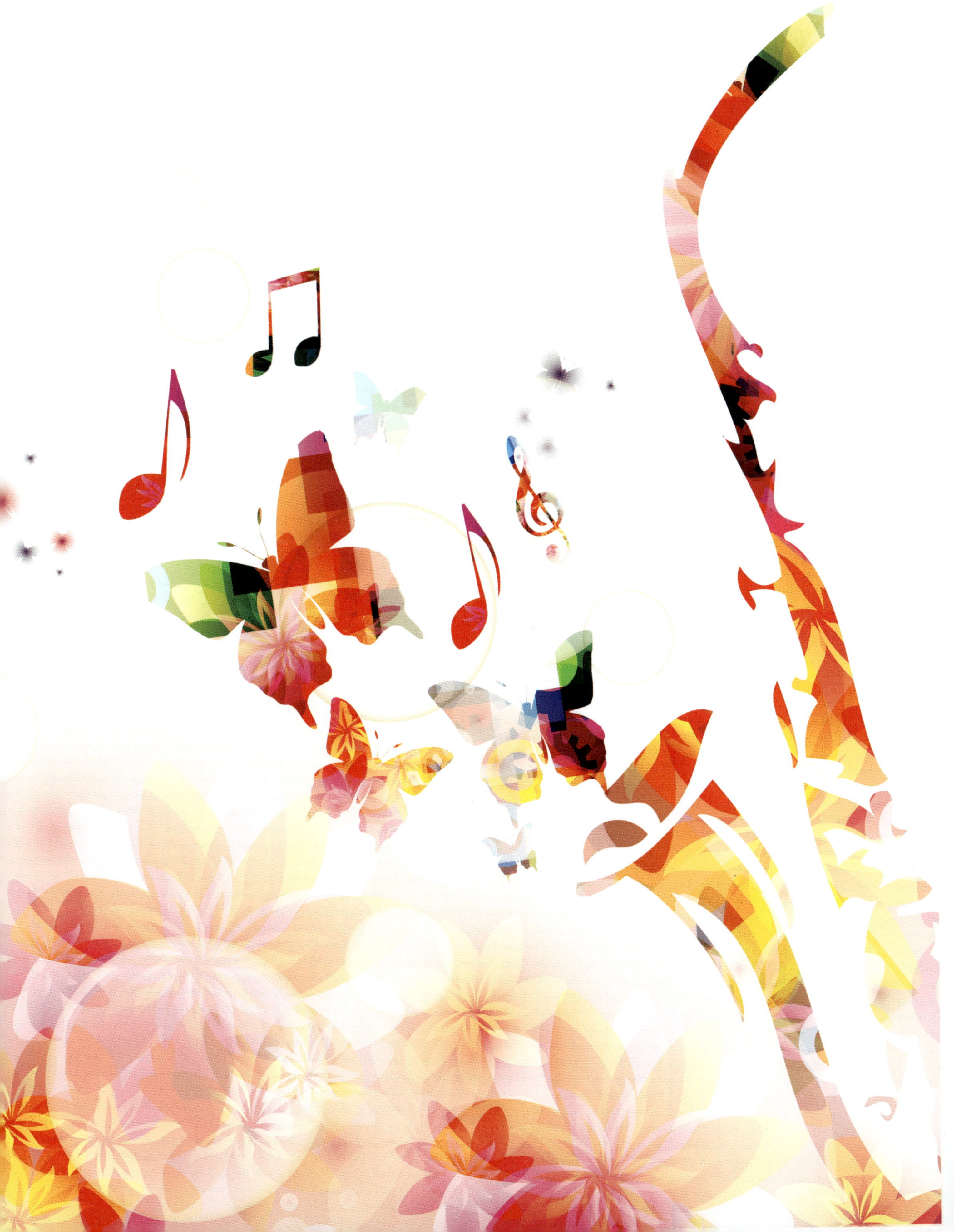

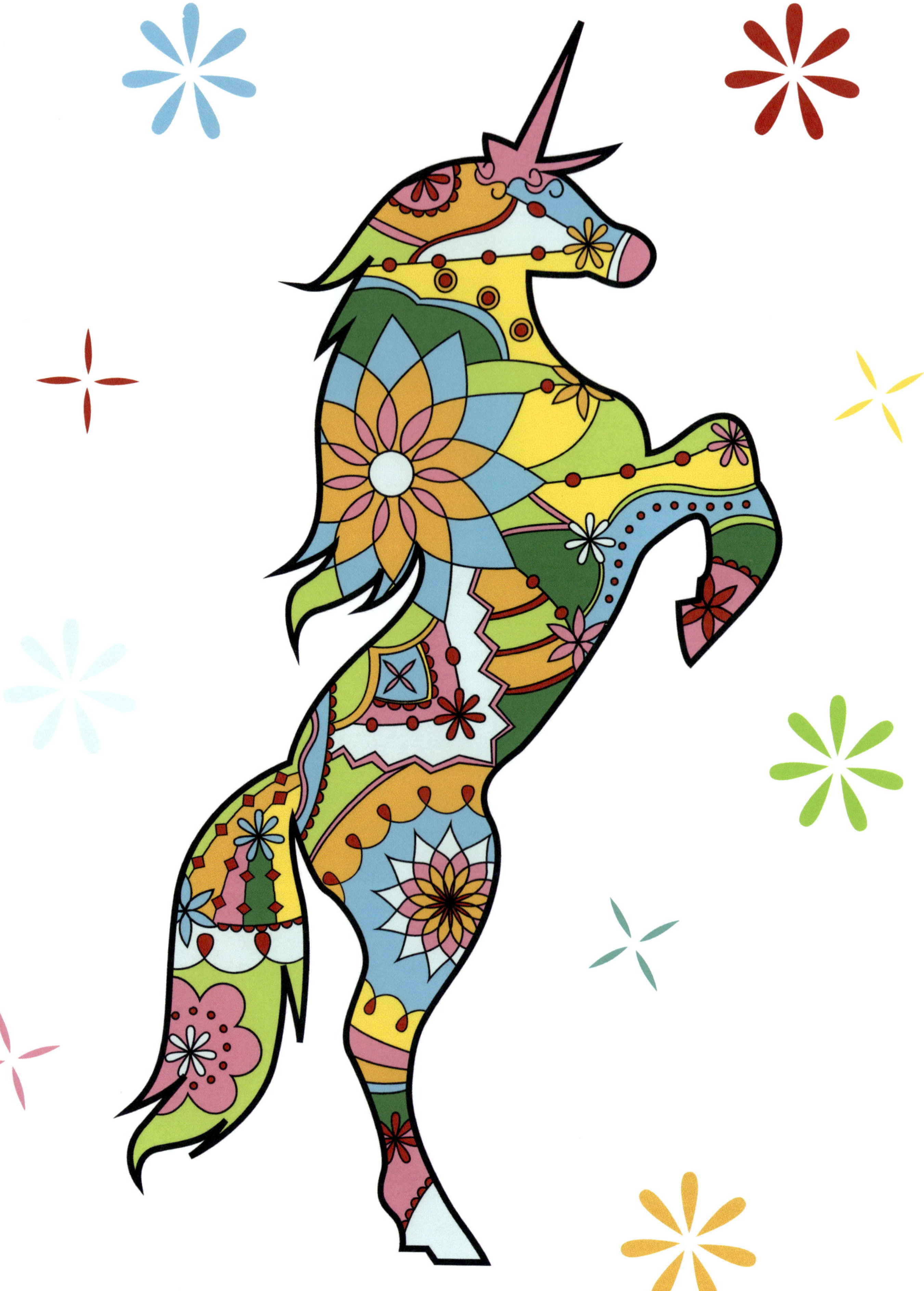

Unicorn Friend

Imagine you are walking in the woods.

It is very quiet.

All you can hear are the sounds of birds . . .

The sound of the wind in the trees . . .

Now imagine that you hear a different sound.

It is the sound of a unicorn playing in the woods.

She looks like a horse with one beautiful horn.

Grownups say that there is no such thing as a unicorn,

But imagine that you are seeing one now, with your very own eyes.

Feeling very safe, you walk up to the unicorn and let her smell your hand.

The unicorn lets you pet her soft fur.

Imagine that the unicorn can talk to you, and you can talk to her, too.

What does she say? What do you tell her?

Imagine you ask the unicorn for a ride, and she says yes.

You gently climb on the unicorn's back, and you explore the forest together.

Where do you go? What do you do?

Do you play in the sunshine?

Do you chase after butterflies?

Do you dance on rainbows?

Now imagine it is time for a nap with the unicorn.

She lies down on the ground, and you rest against her belly, like it's a pillow.

The unicorn gently falls asleep.

You feel her belly go up and down when she breathes.

Now you put your hand on your belly and feel it go up and down as you breathe, too.

Imagine you gently fall asleep with your unicorn friend.

Earth Tour

Let's take a tour of the Earth.

Imagine you go outside and find a comfortable place to relax.

Spread out a small carpet and lie down on it.

Take a deep breath in and out to smell the grass and the flowers.

Listen to the sounds of the birds singing and the wind blowing the leaves in the trees.

Now imagine that your carpet is a flying carpet.

It will take you anywhere in the world.

Feeling very safe, imagine flying to the beach.

You float over the beach and take a deep breath in and out.

You hear the songs of seabirds, and you taste salt in the air.

Now imagine flying your carpet to the mountains.

Let your flying carpet float over the top of a mountain.

Take a deep breath in and out.

Smell the pine trees and listen to the sound of a soaring hawk.

Now imagine that you fly your carpet to the desert.

Floating over the desert, take a deep breath in and out.

Feel the dry, warm air inside your nose, and hear the sound of a hummingbird's wings.

Now let your flying carpet travel to any other place on Earth you would like to visit.

What do you see? What do you smell?

What do you hear? What do you taste?

What do you feel?

Now fly your carpet back to your resting spot in the grass.

Feel the ground below your back, holding you and supporting you.

Send love and thanks to the Earth for being our beautiful home.

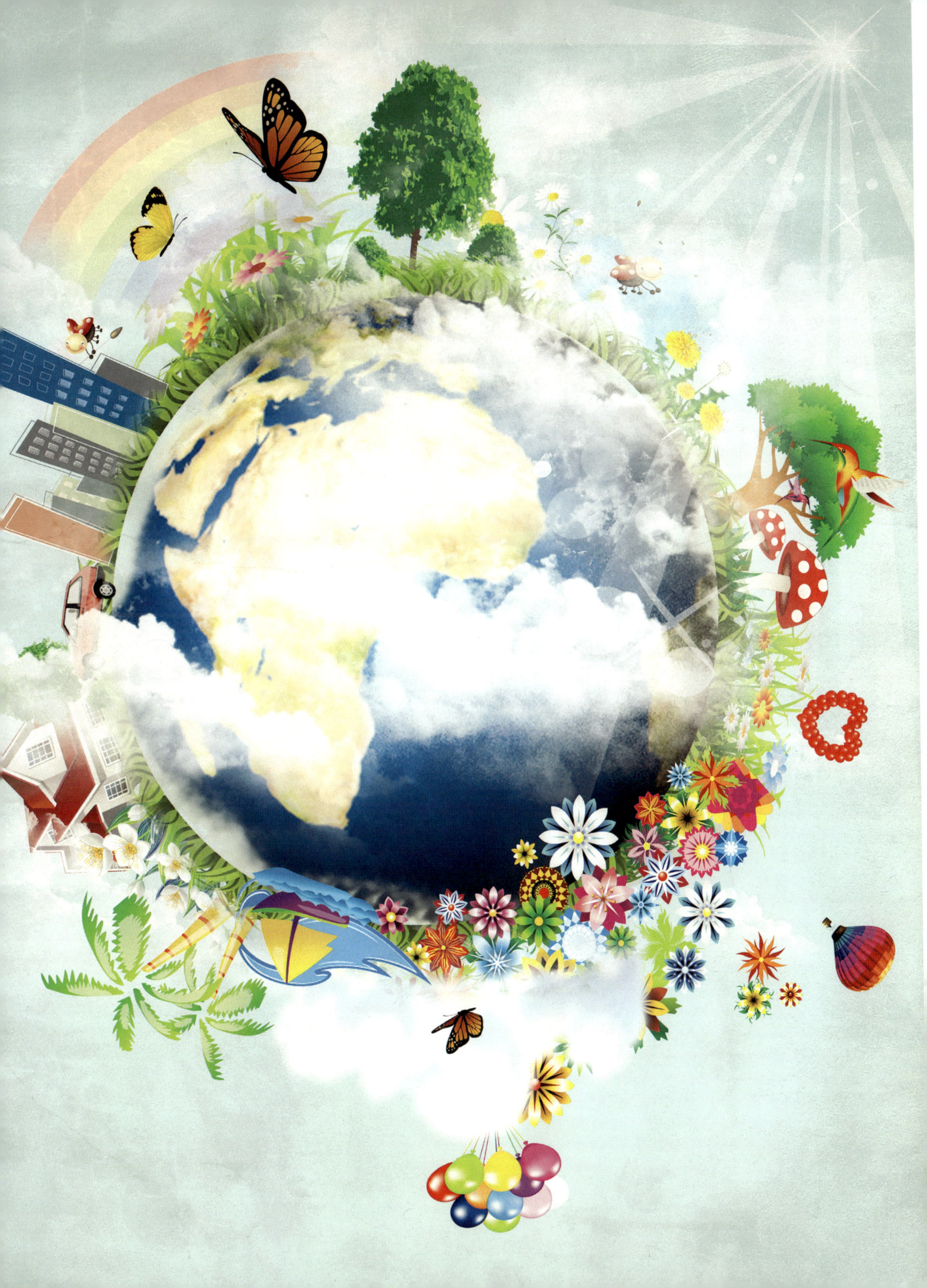

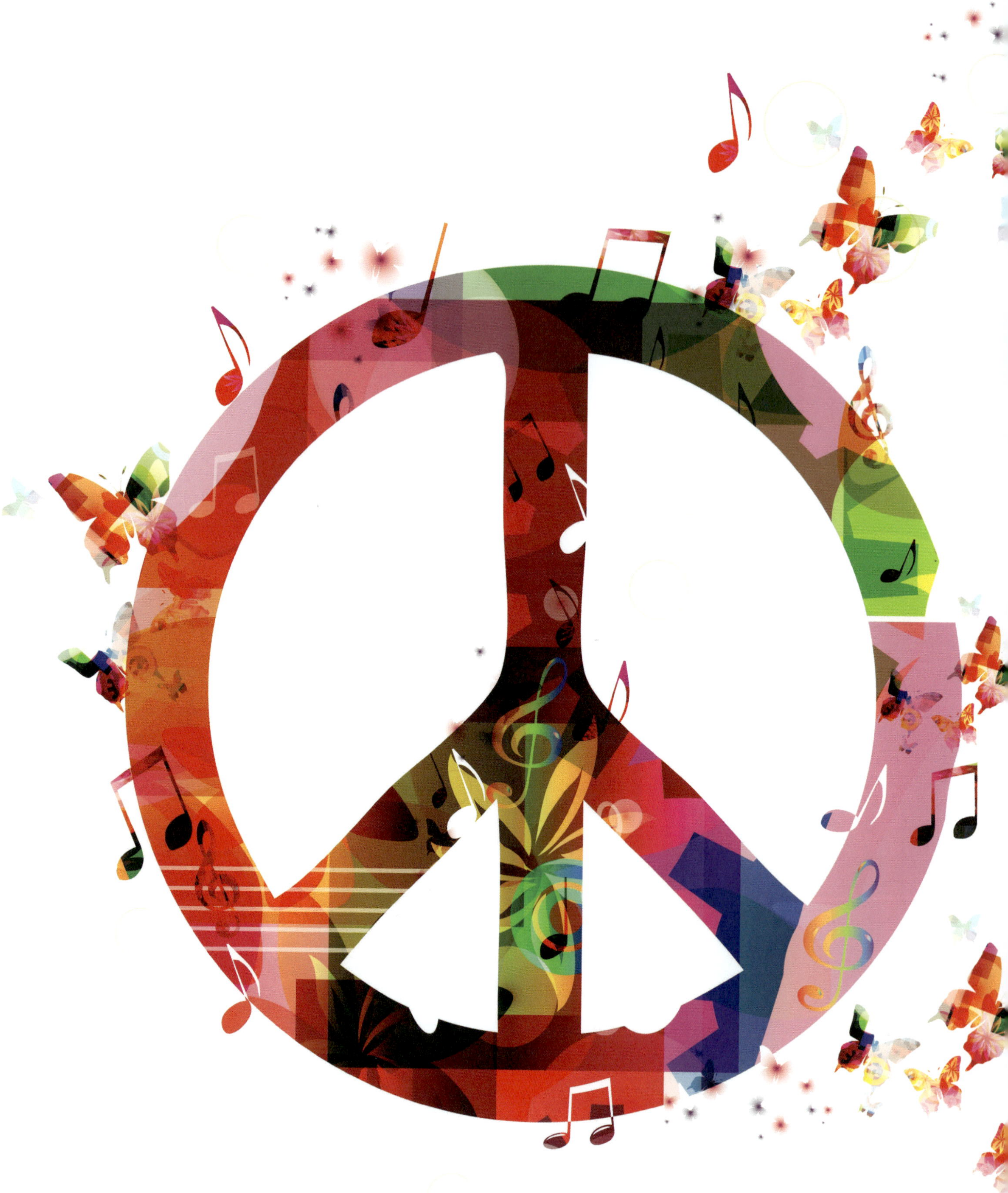

Peaceful Body, Peaceful World

Imagine peace.

What does it feel like? What does it look like?

What does it sound like? What does it smell like?

What does it taste like?

Now let's send peace to your whole body.

Imagine your legs fill with colorful healing light that brings peace.

Feel your legs, relaxed and peaceful.

Imagine your belly filling with light.

Feel your belly, relaxed and peaceful.

Imagine your heart and lungs filling with light.

Feel your heart and lungs, relaxed and peaceful.

Imagine your arms and hands filling with light.

Feel your arms and hands, relaxed and peaceful.

Imagine your back filling with light.

Feel your back, relaxed and peaceful.

Imagine your whole head filling with light.

Feel your brain, eyes, nose, ears, mouth, and face, relaxed and peaceful.

Imagine your whole body filling with light.

Imagine your whole body is now relaxed, peaceful, and healthy.

Now imagine that you give some of this colorful healing light to a person who is sick.

Imagine that person now feels relaxed and peaceful.

Now imagine giving some of this colorful healing light to every person on Earth.

Imagine that everyone on Earth now feels relaxed, peaceful, and healthy.

The whole planet glows with peace.

More Loving Kindness

NOTE: *This story was originally printed in* Imaginations: Fun Relaxation Stories and Meditations for Kids. *We need more love in the world, and including this story is my way of spreading the love to as many people as possible!*

Imagine that you are sending love to yourself.

Send yourself a valentine that says, "I love you."

Now tell each part of your body that you love it.

"I love you, feet."

"I love you, legs."

"I love you, belly."

"I love you, back."

"I love you, arms."

"I love you, face."

Notice how your body feels when you tell it that you love it.

Now think of someone you love very much—
maybe someone in your family or your best friend.

Send that person some love.

Now think of someone who is mean or unfriendly.

Send this person some love, too.

Sometimes, people are mean because they don't feel loved.

So send this person some extra love.

Now think of all the people all over the world.

Send them some love, too.

Now imagine all of these people you've sent love to.

And now imagine that each of those people sends love back to you.

Feel their love coming back to you.

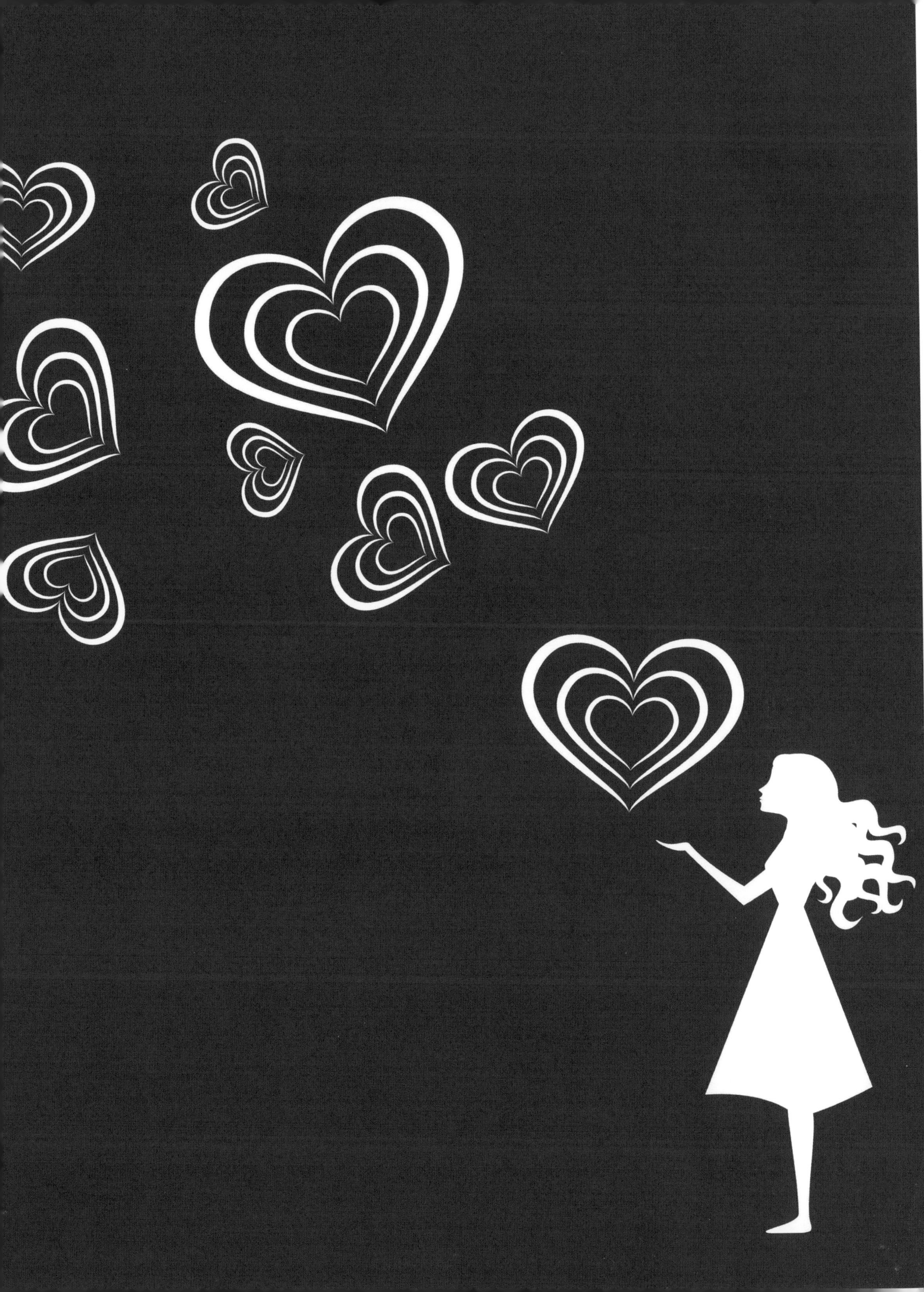

Additional Information and Resources

Looking for more information?

Visit BambinoYoga.com for additional products, resources, activities, and information about relaxation exercises for children.

Loved these stories and want more?

Check out the other books in the Imaginations Series: *Imaginations: Fun Relaxation Stories and Meditations for Kids* and *Imaginations 2: Relaxation Stories and Guided Imagery for Kids*. They both won the San Diego Book Award for Children's Nonfiction! Or visit BambinoYoga.com to download stories and e-books.

Want to listen to audio versions of the guided meditations?

Visit BambinoYoga.com to download audio files or purchase a CD.

Want to keep in touch?

Visit BambinoYoga.com and signup for the newsletter. You'll receive info about relaxation and yoga for kids, as well as contests, sales, and events. You can also like us at Facebook.com/BambinoYoga or follow @BambinoYoga on Twitter.

Want ideas for activities and arts and crafts that correspond with the meditations?

Visit BambinoYoga.com/activities or follow Pinterest.com/BambinoYoga.

Want to help spread the word about this book?

Email info@bambinoyoga.com to share how these stories have helped the children in your life or rate the book on Amazon.com, BN.com, or Goodreads.com to write about your experience. Every review helps create a more relaxed and peaceful world!

Acknowledgements

Thank you to my family for your unending love.

Thank you to Pat Wheeler
and all of the teachers and students
at the Montessori Achievement Centre.

Stefanie Spangler Buswell, thank you for the edits.

Lorie DeWorken, thank you for creating another beautiful book.

Jayden, Addison, Maddux, Hailey, and Rory,
thank you for your beautiful smiles and yoga poses.

And a big thank you to my husband, Drew,
for believing in me and supporting me, always.

Books by Carolyn Clarke

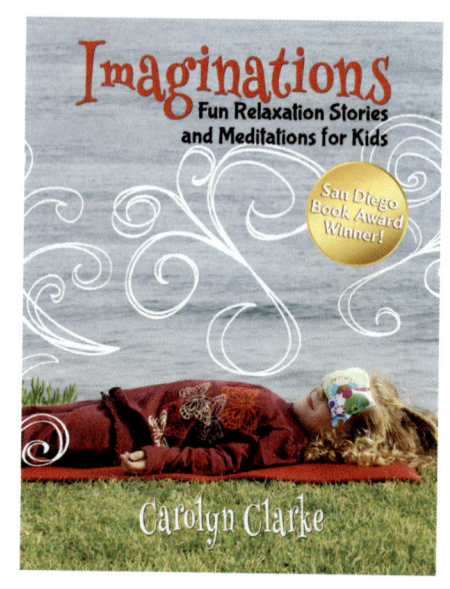

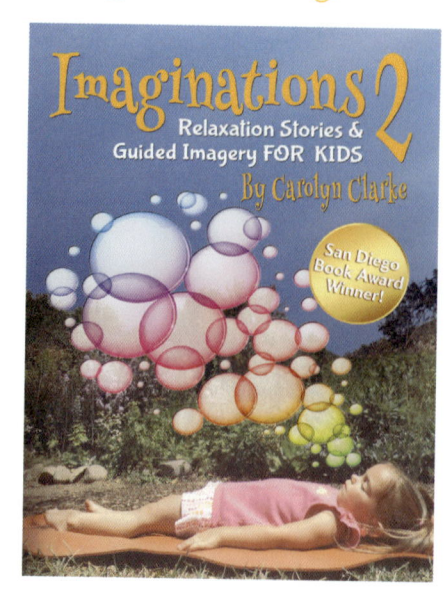

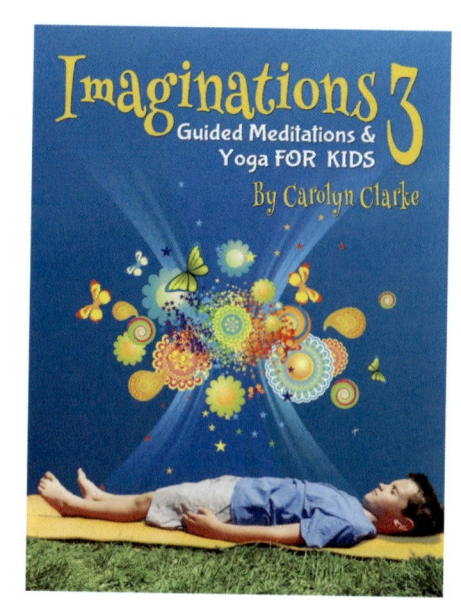

Imaginations: Fun Relaxation Stories and Meditations for Kids

Imaginations 2: Relaxation Stories & Guided Imagery for Kids

Imaginations 3: Guided Meditations & Yoga for Kids

Spanish Translation

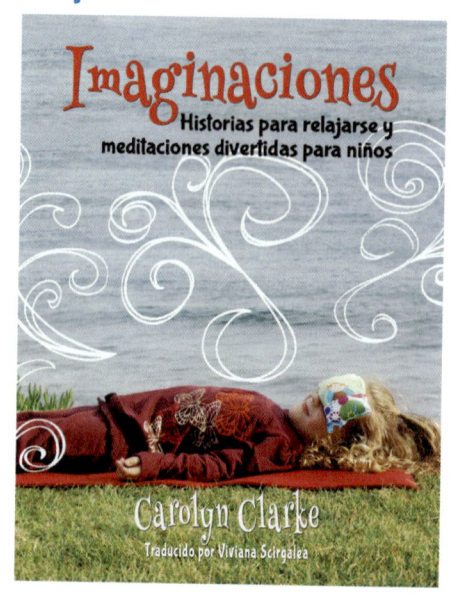

Imaginaciones:
Historias para relajarse y
meditaciones divertidas para niños

Printed in Great Britain
by Amazon